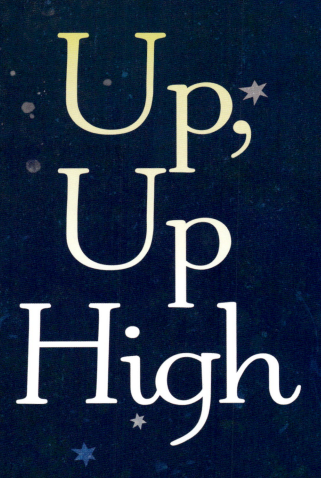

Up, Up, Up High

The Secret Poetry of Earth's Atmosphere

by Lydia Lukidis

illustrated by Katie Rewse

CAPSTONE EDITIONS
a capstone imprint

Published by Capstone Editions, an imprint of Capstone
1710 Roe Crest Drive, North Mankato, Minnesota 56003
capstonepub.com

Text copyright © 2025 by Lydia Lukidis
Illustrations copyright © 2025 by Katie Rewse

All rights reserved. No part of this publication may be reproduced in whole or in part, or
stored in a retrieval system, or transmitted in any form or by any means, electronic, mechanical,
photocopying, recording, or otherwise, without written permission of the publisher.

Library of Congress Cataloging-in-Publication Data is available on the Library of Congress website.
ISBN: 9781630793043 (hardcover)
ISBN: 9781630793067 (ebook PDF)

Summary: Look up—into the blue and beyond. What do you see? The sky—our atmosphere—may
seem empty or invisible. But is it? Using spare, lyrical language, author Lydia Lukidis (*Deep, Deep
Down: The Secret Underwater Poetry of the Mariana Trench*) takes readers on an imagined journey up,
up high to discover the surprising and wondrous things flying, floating, and happening between
the treetops and the stars in this awe-inspiring STEM-based picture book.

Designed by Jaime Willems

Printed and bound in China. PO 6096

For my parents and daughter, my three rocks on this life journey, thank you for loving me unconditionally.
—L.L.

For Jack and Harry, reach for the stars
—K.R.

Up,
up,
high,
higher than the tallest trees,
higher than the biggest buildings,
floats an invisible world—
Earth's atmosphere.

Do air and clouds dominate the massive sky?
Does anything else exist up there?
Where does the sky end
and space begin?

To find out,
squeeze into a space suit.
Strap yourself
into a spacecraft.

Modern spacecrafts take off vertically and land with parachutes either in the ocean or on land. They can travel around Earth at a speed of about 17,500 miles (28,000 kilometers) per hour. That is about 35 times faster than a commercial airplane!

altitude: 1.5 miles (2.4 km)
atmospheric layer: troposphere

As you fly
up,
up,
up,
the spacecraft pierces
cotton-candy clouds.

The air pressure drops,
and oxygen levels
plummet
     down,
        down,
           down.

A bone-chilling cold
blasts through the air.

Altitude is the height of an object above sea level. High altitude starts at 8,000 feet (2,438 meters). As altitude rises, air pressure—the weight of air pressing down—drops. There are two reasons for this. First, gravity pulls the air as close to Earth's surface as possible. Second, the higher up you go, the fewer gas molecules there are. The air becomes thin and less dense.

altitude: 5.5 miles (8.9 km)
atmospheric layer: troposphere

Peek out the window. What do you see?

At 29,035 feet (8,850 m) Mount Everest, located in the Himalayas, is the highest point on Earth. Temperatures can plummet to minus 76 degrees Fahrenheit (minus 60 degrees Celsius). Despite this, different animals, including snow leopards and Himalayan jumping spiders, call this mountain home. When altitude reaches 26,000 feet (7,925 m), it is called the death zone. This area is ruled by raging winds and less breathable oxygen. Some people still attempt to climb the mountain, but they must use oxygen tanks and dress warmly in order to survive.

Tufts of snow sparkle
on shards of gray limestone
as you soar past the very top
of majestic Mount Everest,
the highest point on Earth.

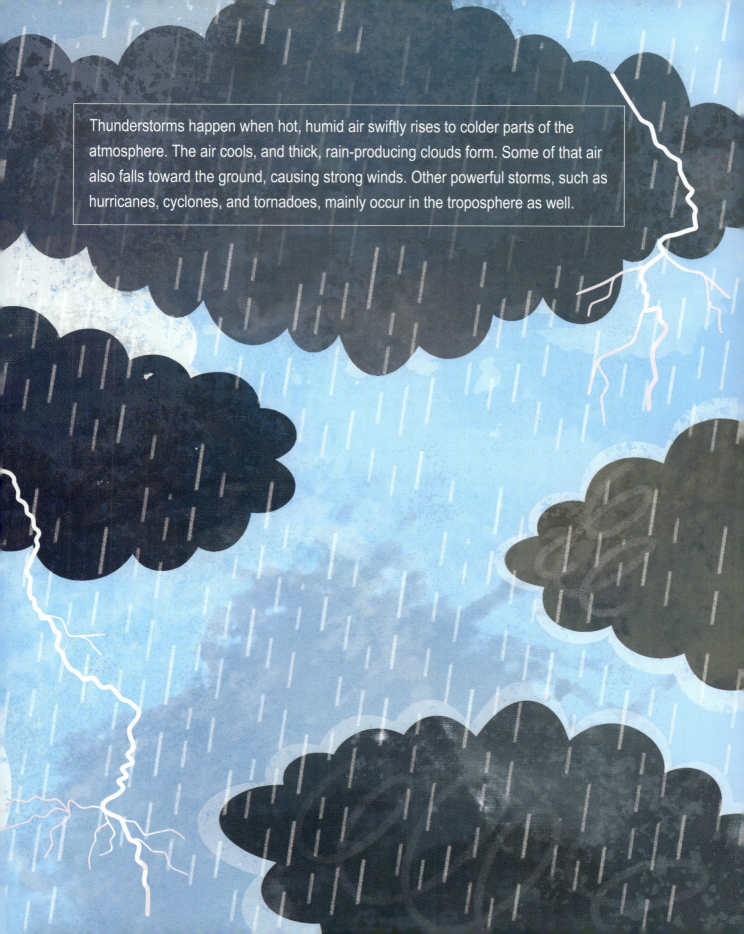

Thunderstorms happen when hot, humid air swiftly rises to colder parts of the atmosphere. The air cools, and thick, rain-producing clouds form. Some of that air also falls toward the ground, causing strong winds. Other powerful storms, such as hurricanes, cyclones, and tornadoes, mainly occur in the troposphere as well.

altitude: 21.7 miles (34.9 km)
atmospheric layer: stratosphere

Seconds later,
the storm clouds disappear.

You continue rising
in the sky.

A flash of white
floats by.

You press up against
the window to witness
a weather balloon
dancing and
   drifting
          through the atmosphere.

Each day, 1,800 weather balloons from around the world float up into the atmosphere. They help predict the weather. The balloons carry a small instrument called a radiosonde. This battery-powered radio hangs below and sends information to a ground receiver. As the balloon floats through the atmosphere, it measures pressure, temperature, and humidity. When the balloon goes beyond its limit . . . *POP!* It bursts. A parachute opens, and the radiosonde safely returns to Earth to be used again.

altitude: 25.3 miles (40.7 km)
atmospheric layer: stratosphere

Up,
up
high
you zoom.

Minutes later,
you spot
a man in a space suit.

He steps forward,
    waves,
        then jumps!

Watch
as he plummets
   down,
      down,
         down,
speeding,
spinning,
spiraling
through the atmosphere.

Space jumping is an adventurous yet dangerous sport. Jumpers leap from a spacecraft or balloon and fall toward Earth. Most skydivers jump from about 10,000 feet (3,000 m). But in 2014, 58-year-old computer scientist and engineer Alan Eustace set a new world record. Using a helium-filled balloon, he ascended nearly 26 miles (42 km) above Earth's surface—then jumped. It only took 14 minutes and 27 seconds for Eustace to return to Earth. At one point, he reached a speed of 822 miles (1,323 km) per hour—faster than the speed of sound!

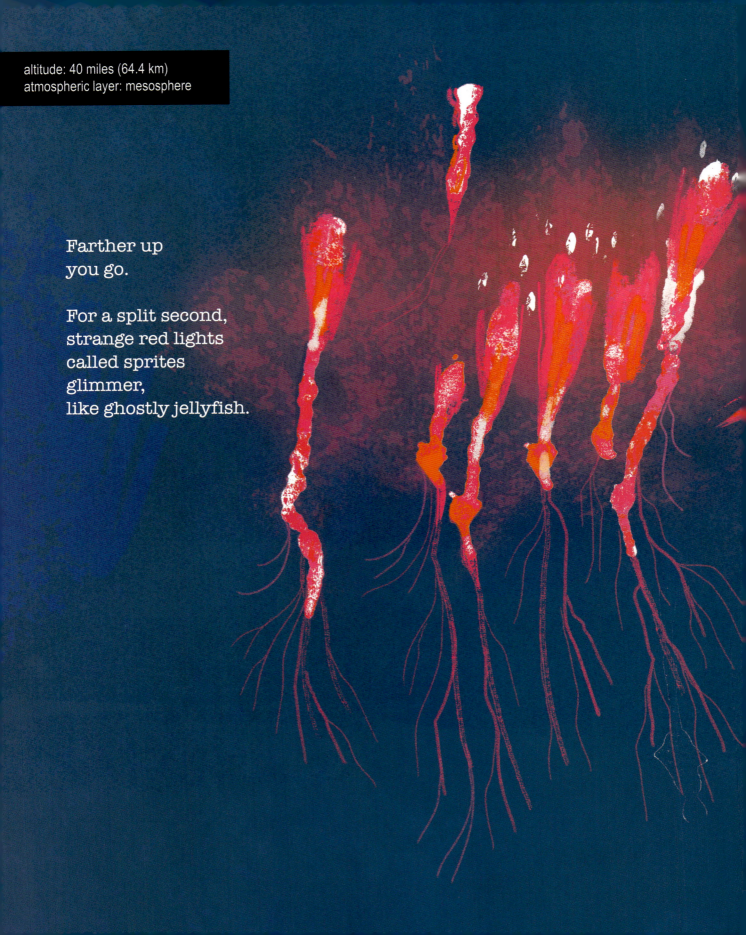

altitude: 40 miles (64.4 km)
atmospheric layer: mesosphere

Farther up
you go.

For a split second,
strange red lights
called sprites
glimmer,
like ghostly jellyfish.

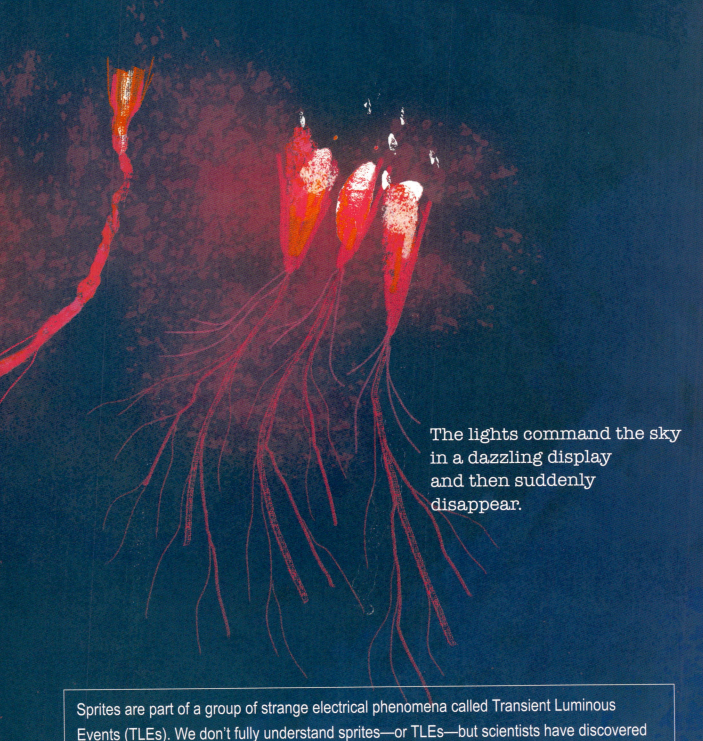

The lights command the sky in a dazzling display and then suddenly disappear.

Sprites are part of a group of strange electrical phenomena called Transient Luminous Events (TLEs). We don't fully understand sprites—or TLEs—but scientists have discovered they occur above active thunderstorms. They appear right after lightning streaks from a cloud to the ground. Sprites flash for less than a tenth of a second and then disappear. They aren't very bright and can only be seen at night using highly sensitive cameras.

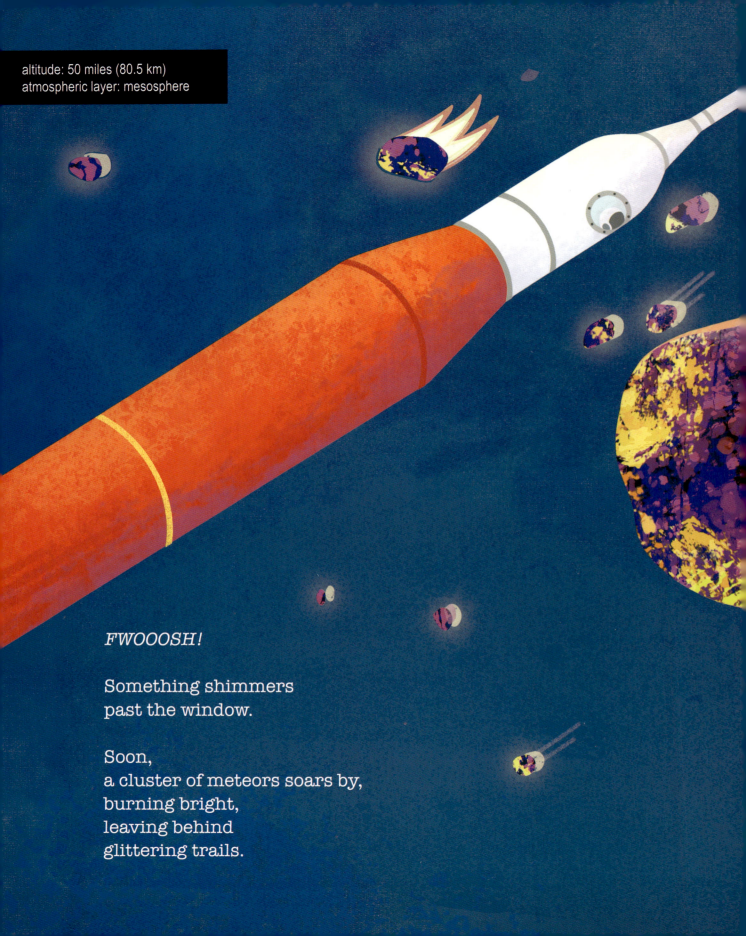

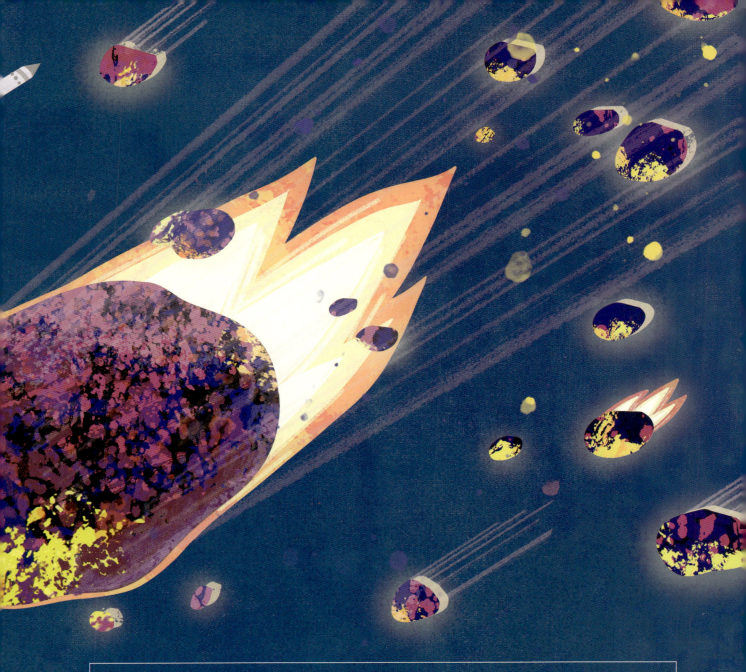

Meteoroids are lumps of rock or iron from space. When they enter Earth's atmosphere, we call them meteors. They usually burn up completely and create bright streaks. From Earth, they may look like shooting stars. But some bigger meteors don't completely burn up in the atmosphere. They make it all the way to our planet. We call these meteor*ites*. So far, the largest meteorite ever found is the Hoba meteorite. It was discovered in Namibia, a country in Africa, and weighed 145,505 pounds (66,000 kilograms). That's the weight of about 17 elephants!

The Aurora Borealis (Northern Lights) and Aurora Australis (Southern Lights) are natural displays of colored lights. They occur in the night sky near the North and South Poles. What causes these displays? Earth is surrounded and protected by a system of magnetic fields. These fields help deflect solar wind—energy from the sun traveling to Earth. Most solar wind is deflected away, but some particles are attracted to the North and South Poles, where the magnetic fields are weaker. The particles collide with the upper reaches of our atmosphere and cause various gases to glow in different colors and create twinkling lights.

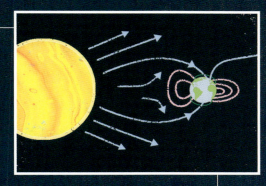

Waves of blue,
    yellow,
        and green
merge together like magic,
shimmering
and shifting
in a sea of color.

altitude: 248 miles (400 km)
atmospheric layer: thermosphere

As you rise
higher and higher,
Earth looks
smaller and smaller.
What seemed like a flat surface
slowly stretches out,
its edges curving,
disappearing,
as if they're melting away.

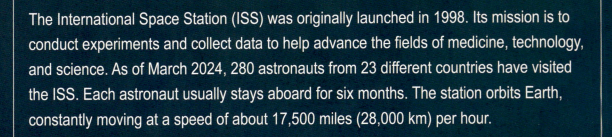

The International Space Station (ISS) was originally launched in 1998. Its mission is to conduct experiments and collect data to help advance the fields of medicine, technology, and science. As of March 2024, 280 astronauts from 23 different countries have visited the ISS. Each astronaut usually stays aboard for six months. The station orbits Earth, constantly moving at a speed of about 17,500 miles (28,000 km) per hour.

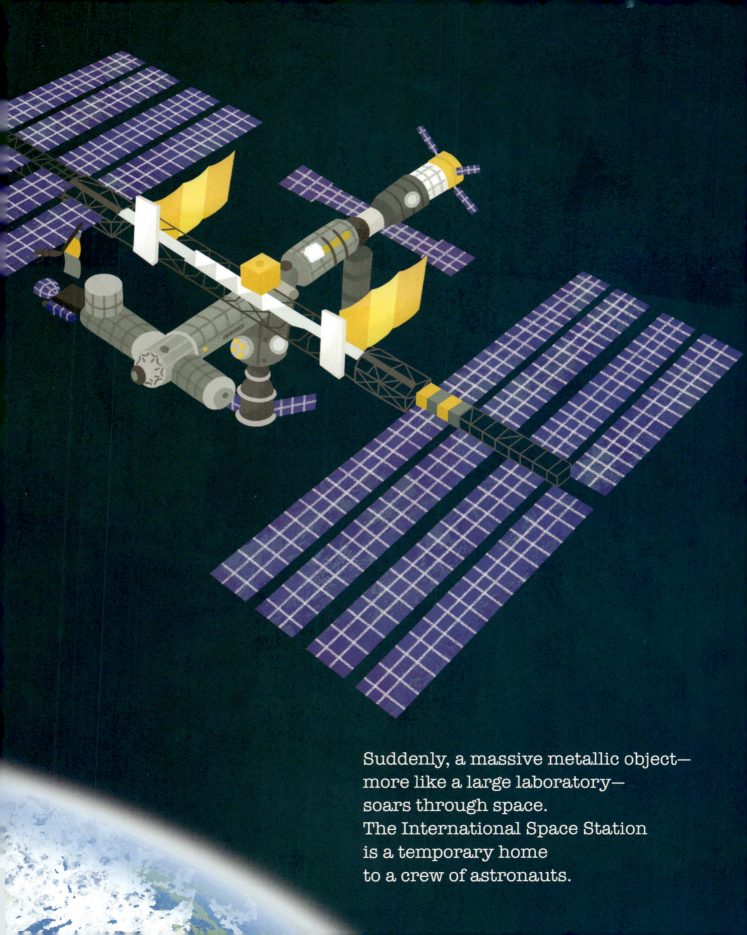

Suddenly, a massive metallic object—
more like a large laboratory—
soars through space.
The International Space Station
is a temporary home
to a crew of astronauts.

altitude: 434.9 miles (700 km)
atmospheric layer: exosphere

Your spacecraft sails silently.

A smiling face floats by.

In 1961, Russian astronaut Yuri Gagarin became the first human to ever journey to space. Since then, hundreds of astronauts have made the trip aboard various spacecrafts. Once in orbit, crews see a sunrise or sunset every 90 minutes.

An astronaut!
She drifts,
    twists,
        glides
through space gracefully
as she conducts experiments
near her spacecraft.

altitude: 1,242.7 miles (2,000 km)
atmospheric layer: exosphere

Rise higher and higher
and watch as the atmosphere grows
dimmer,
darker.

Light fades away
until . . .
a flash of silver
whizzes by!

Thousands of satellites are currently orbiting Earth. Some help
with communication, sending information back to Earth to be
used on devices including phones, televisions, and radios.
Others are used for navigation and GPS mapping or to help
predict the weather. Satellites can orbit our planet without falling
down because they're set at speeds fast enough to defeat the
downward pull of gravity.

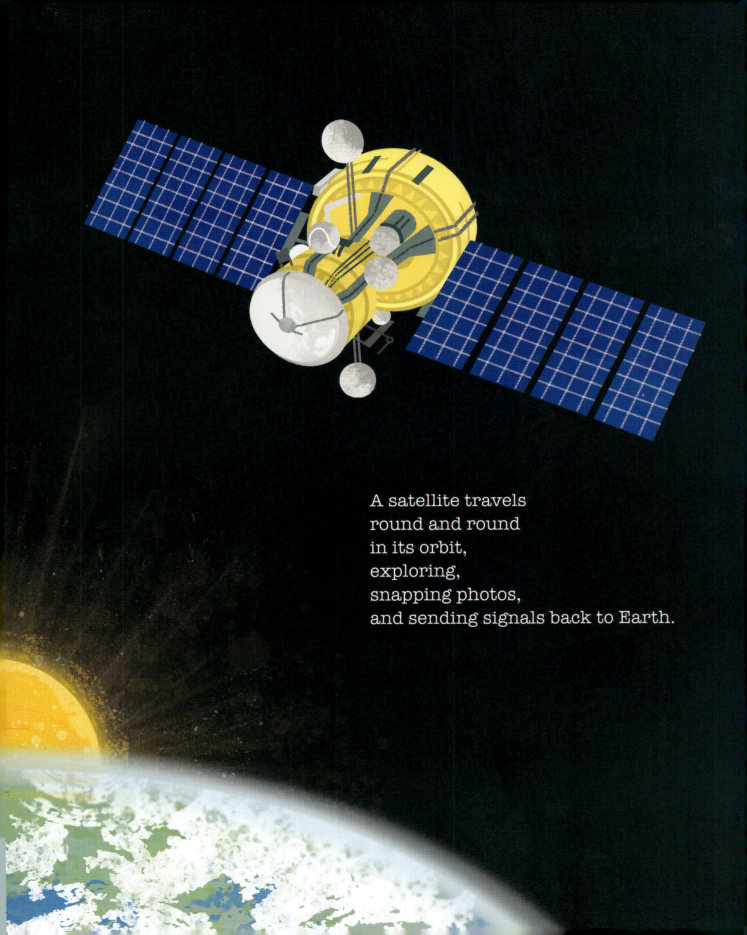

A satellite travels
round and round
in its orbit,
exploring,
snapping photos,
and sending signals back to Earth.

altitude: 7,000 miles (11,265.4 km)
beyond Earth's atmosphere: outer space

From space, Earth's atmosphere appears like a thin, glowing band surrounding the entire planet. During a sunrise or sunset, the part closest to Earth is orange, and then the color changes to brown, gray, blue, until it fades into the black of space. It's not really the atmosphere we're seeing—it's different gases. We see different colors because the main gases and particles in each layer act as prisms. When light passes through, the different wavelengths—or colors—separate or bend in different ways.

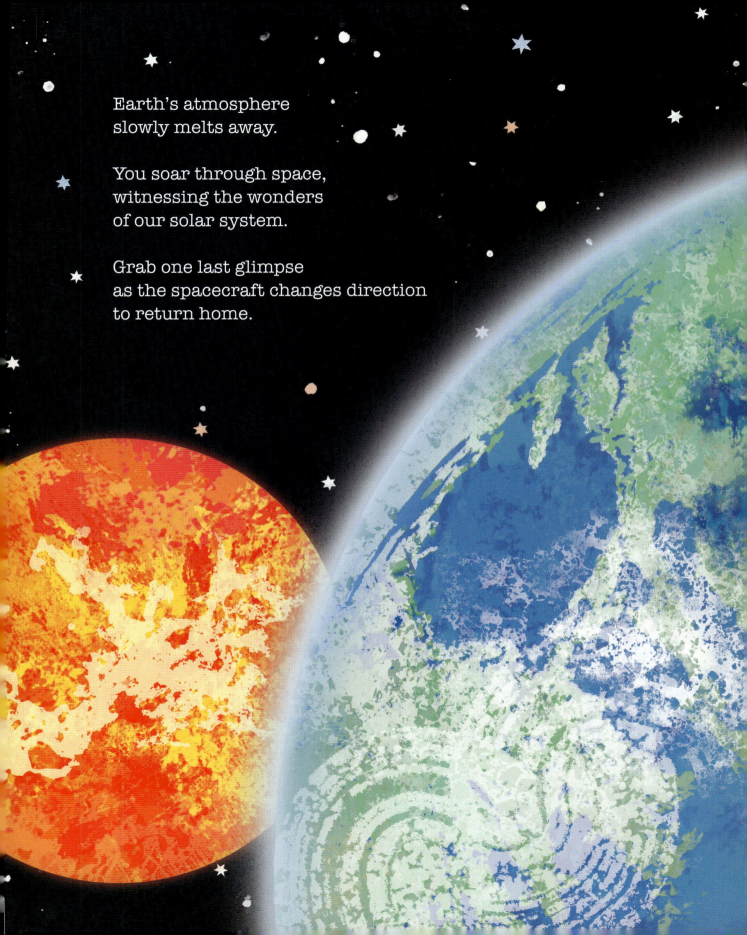

Earth's atmosphere slowly melts away.

You soar through space, witnessing the wonders of our solar system.

Grab one last glimpse as the spacecraft changes direction to return home.

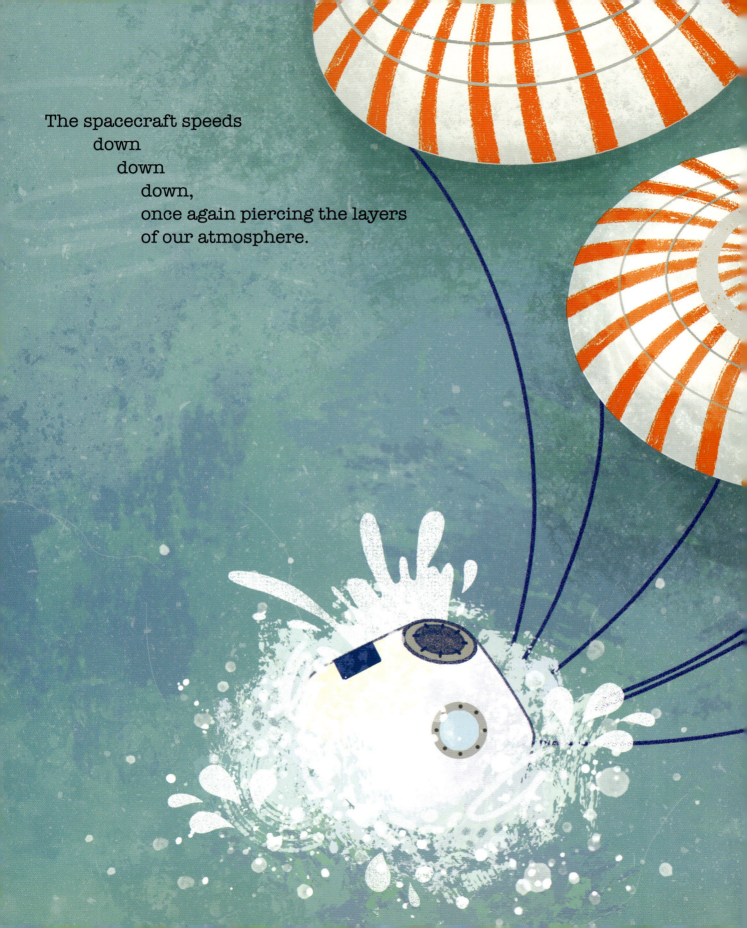

The spacecraft speeds
   down
     down
       down,
       once again piercing the layers
       of our atmosphere.

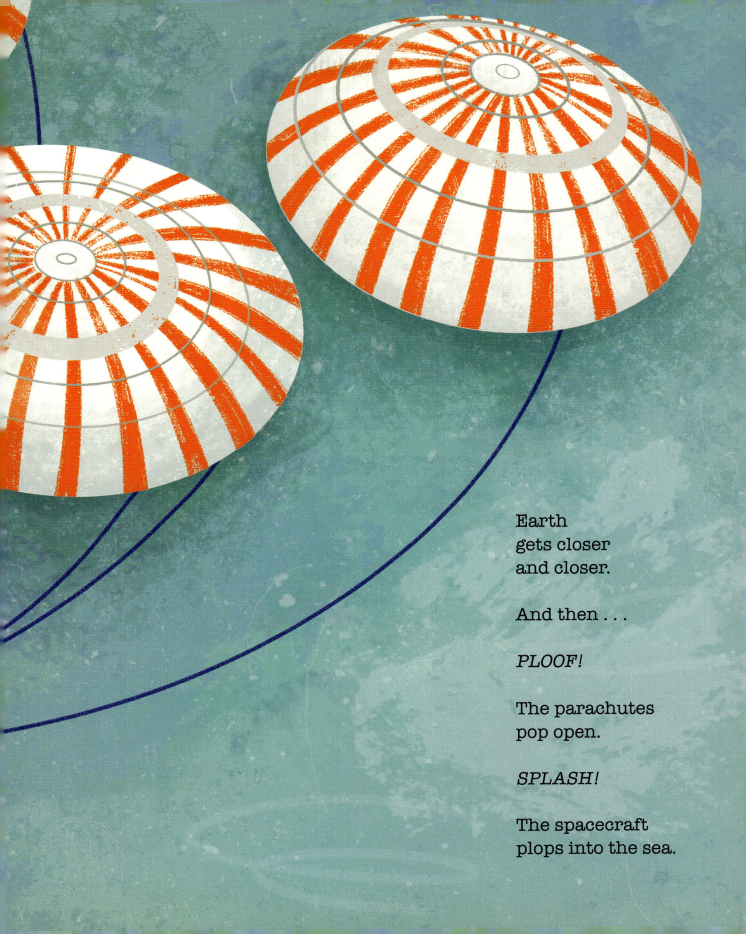

Earth gets closer and closer.

And then . . .

PLOOF!

The parachutes pop open.

SPLASH!

The spacecraft plops into the sea.

Your feet are once again
planted on the ground.

But as you gaze
up,
up
high,
remember the invisible world above.

Earth's atmosphere—
   sometimes a chaotic battlefield,
      sometimes a magical playground—
   always protecting us,
   forever giving us life.

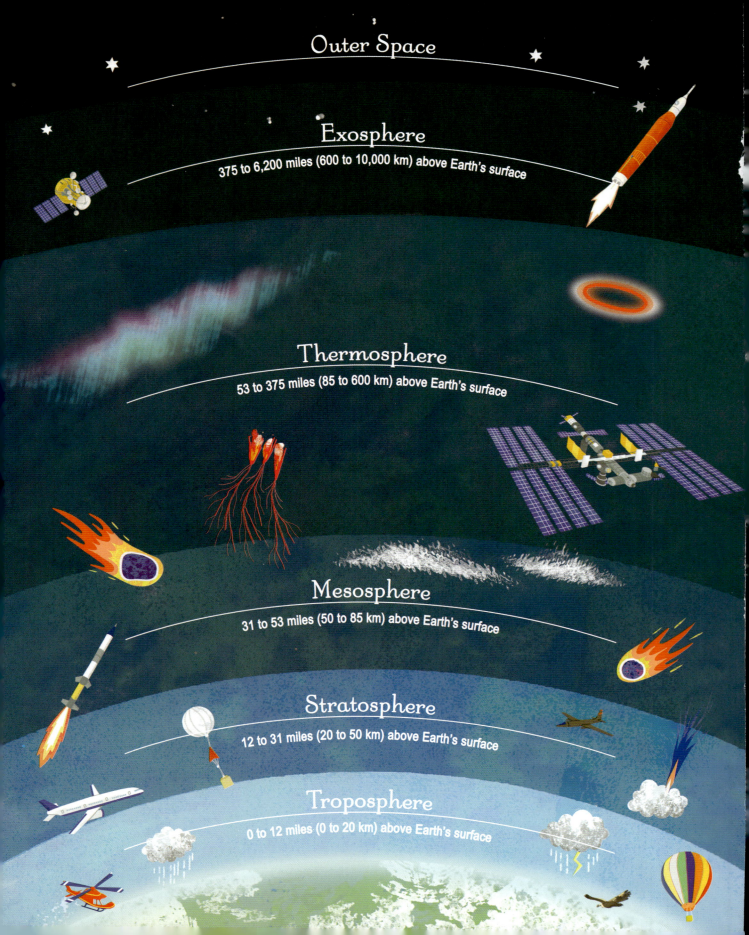

Earth's Atmosphere

Up, up high lies an invisible world. Earth's atmosphere is a sea of gas that surrounds our entire planet, held in place by gravity. It not only protects us from harmful rays but also gives us life. Life on Earth wouldn't exist without it! The atmosphere includes five different layers:

The **EXOSPHERE** is the highest and least defined layer. The air is extremely thin, and there's no oxygen. It's almost a perfect vacuum, meaning it's almost empty. The exosphere gradually fades away into outer space.

- **Temperature**—The actual temperature in this layer can't be measured by a thermometer because the air is extremely thin with few air particles and low density. But it can range from extremely hot to extremely cold, depending on solar activity.
- **What can you see?** high-Earth orbit satellites, spacecrafts, and space stations

The **THERMOSPHERE** is the thickest layer in the atmosphere. Gravity changes and space travelers begin to experience weightlessness.

- **Temperature**—This is the hottest atmospheric layer. That is because high-energy ultraviolet and X-ray radiation from the sun are absorbed by the molecules in this layer. It can get as hot as 3,600°F (2,000°C) near the top.
- **What can you see?** spacecrafts, space stations, Aurora Borealis and Aurora Australis, some low-Earth orbit satellites, research rockets, and some space stations (including the International Space Station)

The **MESOSPHERE** is a bit of a mystery. It's too high for most aircrafts and weather balloons but too low for spacecrafts. Many strange electrical discharges, including TLEs, also occur here.

- **Temperature**—The higher you go, the colder it gets. Temperatures at the bottom start at 5°F (−15°C) and drop to −130°F (−90°C) at the top. It is the coldest part of Earth's atmosphere.
- **What can you see?** high-altitude clouds, meteorological rockets, meteors burning up, research rockets, rocket-powered aircrafts, and some types of TLEs

The **STRATOSPHERE** is much calmer. There are jet streams—narrow bands of strong wind—in the lower part. Many commercial airplanes fly here in order to avoid the turbulence.

- **Temperature**—In this layer, it gets warmer the higher you go. Temperatures reach a maximum of 5°F (−15°C) at the top.
- **What can you see?** weather balloons and radiosondes, commercial and jet planes, spy planes, some clouds, some types of TLEs, and space jumpers

The **TROPOSPHERE** can be a chaotic battlefield! Most weather occurs here, and conditions tend to change suddenly and violently. The troposphere holds most of the oxygen we, along with plants and animals, need to survive.

- **Temperature**—The troposphere starts off with an average temperature of 62°F (17°C). But the higher you go, the colder it gets. It drops to −60°F (−51°C).
- **What can you see?** Rüppell's griffon vultures (the world's highest flying bird), some mountains (including Mount Everest), volcanoes, some commercial airplanes, hot air balloons, helicopters, most clouds, skydivers, and almost all weather

Note: The listed temperatures and distances are estimations and depend on factors such as solar radiation or the amount of sunlight. The atmosphere is also lower at both the North and South Poles.

Acknowledgments

Sincere thanks to Dr. Zhang at the Cooperative Institute for Research in Environmental Sciences (CIRES) at the University of Colorado Boulder, and to Alan Eustace.

Glossary

air pressure (AIR PRESH-ur)—force exerted by the weight of the molecules that make up air; usually, the lower the air pressure, the stronger the storm

altitude (AL-ti-tood)—the height of something above sea level or Earth's surface

atmosphere (AT-muhss-feer)—the layer of gases that surrounds a planet

gravity (GRAV-uh-tee)—a force that pulls objects with mass together; gravity pulls objects down toward the center of Earth

orbit (OR-bit)—the path an object follows as it goes around the sun or a planet

prism (PRIH-zum)—a glass or transparent object with flat surfaces that refracts and separates white light into a spectrum of colors

solar radiation (SOH-lur ray-dee-AY-shuhn)—the sunlight and energy that comes from the sun

Read More

Lukidis, Lydia. *Deep, Deep Down: The Secret Underwater Poetry of the Mariana Trench.* North Mankato, MN: Capstone Editions, 2023.

McAnulty, Stacy. *Our Planet!: There's No Place Like Earth.* New York: Henry Holt and Company, 2022.

Wargula, Doris. *Earth's Atmosphere.* Buffalo, NY: Britannica Educational Publishing, 2025.

Internet Sites

NASA: International Space Station
nasa.gov/international-space-station/

NASA: NASA Kids' Club
nasa.gov/learning-resources/nasa-kids-club/

NASA: NASA Kids Science
science.nasa.gov/kids/

National Weather Service: Resources for Kids
weather.gov/hun/outreach_kids_corner

NOAA National Severe Storms Laboratory: Learning Resources: For Students
nssl.noaa.gov/education/students/

About the Author

Lydia Lukidis is an award-winning author of more than 50 trade and educational books for children. Her titles include *Deep, Deep, Down: The Secret Underwater Poetry of the Mariana Trench* (Capstone Editions, 2023)—a Crystal Kite Award winner, a 2024 Forest of Reading Honour Book (Ontario Library Association), and a Cybils Award nominee—as well as *Dancing Through Space: Dr. Mae Jemison Soars to New Heights* (Albert Whitman & Company, 2024). A resident of Quebec, Canada, and a science enthusiast from a young age, Lydia now incorporates her scientific studies and everlasting curiosity into her books. Visit her website at lydialukidis.com.

photo credit: Magenta Photo

About the Illustrator

Katie Rewse is an illustrator based in Cornwall, England. She studied for both her BA and MA in illustration at the Arts University Bournemouth and, since graduating in 2017, has specialized in children's book illustration. In 2020, Katie was shortlisted in the AOI World Illustration Awards, and in 2021, the nonfiction title *Climate Action*, which Katie illustrated, was longlisted for the Blue Peter Book Awards and was a Waterstone's Children's Book of the Month. *Climate Action* also won a Green Earth Book Award in 2022.

Katie is particularly interested in how illustration can be used to inspire positive change and she finds inspiration in the outdoors, travel, and adventure.